AUGUST EVENING
WITH TRUMPET

AUGUST EVENING WITH TRUMPET

POEMS BY

HARRY HUMES

The University of Arkansas Press
Fayetteville
2004

Copyright © 2004 by The University of Arkansas Press

All rights reserved
Manufactured in Korea by Pacifica Communications
08 07 06 05 04   5 4 3 2 1

Designed by Liz Lester

∞ The paper used in this publication meets the mini-
mum requirements of the American National Standard
for Permanence of Paper for Printed Library Materials
Z39.48-1984.

LIBRARY OF CONGRESS
CATALOGING-IN-PUBLICATION DATA

Humes, Harry.
    August evening with trumpet : poems /
by Harry Humes.
        p.   cm.
    ISBN 1-55728-774-0 (pbk. : alk. paper)
    I. Title.
PS3558.U444A95 2004
811'.54—dc22
                                    2004006307

For my wife, Nancy,
and my daughters, Leah and Rachel,
and my brother Bill

ACKNOWLEDGMENTS

I am grateful to the editors of the following magazines in which these poems first appeared:

"Dance Hall," *Antietam Review;* "Trout Are Moving," *Beloit Poetry Journal;* "String," "The Movement of Ice," *Descant;* "Landscape with Olga," *Hampden-Sydney Poetry Review;* "Walking by the Ocean," *Hollins Critic;* "Why Not Swim Out," *Mad Poets;* "Edward Hopper's Women," *Poet Lore;* "Clam Gatherer," "The Visit," "Late November," "Antler Tree," "August Evening with Trumpet," "A Theory," "Porch," *Poetry Northwest;* "Nature," "Gravel Song" (as "Tycho Brahe's Love Song"), *Quarterly West;* "Tent Sleep," *Salmagundi;* "Hand-Me-Downs," *Salt Hill;* "Throwing Away the Compass," *Shenandoah;* "Leah in the Outfield," *Sport Literate;* "Lee & Melissa, Always," "Crab Lines," *Tar River Poetry;* "New Dark," "The Mountains," *The Journal;* "An Irruption of Birds," "Plowed Fields in January," *Two Rivers Review;* "Fishing at Dusk," *Washington Square;* "Guests," "The Relocation of Rattlesnakes," "Game," "The Stillness," "Evolution," "The River Is Quiet Tonight," *West Branch.*

I am indebted to Bruce Weigl and his poem "What Saves Us" for some of the language in my "Landscape with Olga."

The poem "Small History of a House" is loosely based on a personal experience related to me by Richard Savage.

Additionally, I would like to thank the following:

Rich Ives, Rodger Moody, and Phil Memmer, editors of small presses in whose limited-edition books several of the above poems have appeared.

And my good friends Dan Donaghy, Paul Martin, and Bruce Weigl, all of whom read the poems in the manuscript and offered valuable suggestions.

And special thanks to my editor, Enid Shomer, for her wonderful fishing stories and for her close final reading of my work.

CONTENTS

String

I found it zig-zagging hundreds of yards
through woods, tangled in understory,
maybe a hunter's way to his stand,
or else the work of someone
who woke in the middle of the night,
and without disturbing his wife
walked into the dark with a ball of string
knotted together from pieces
he'd saved for years,
playing it out behind him
perhaps for the sweet confusion,
the imp loose in him,
a string trail to nowhere
that wind rippled
and gray birds perched on,
though there was something human
its entire length,
the cinch and blood knots,
the tramped places where he hesitated,
cigarette butt or candy wrapper,
moonlight streaming over him,
joy or melancholy in him,
letting string slip through his fingers,
feeling its hum, its lack of direction
possibly the only direction
he could think to leave behind.

TENT SLEEP

It depends on light and stream murmur,
and the little pockets inside
for knife and compass, and whether
the moon is yellow or white,
and how many stars glitter between
the branches of spruce and birch.
Also twig snap and leaf rustle,
embers in the fire ring
like a city a long way off.
Feather smell and ripple
of fabric, and remembered tents
of childhood, rugs thrown over
a clothesline, corners anchored with rocks—
that is the sleep that comes easing in
through the whole round dark
pressing down on everything.

THE MOUNTAINS

This is where we forget rooms
and windows, this place of old shirts
and boots where even at hottest noon
there is always the thought
of snow behind tansy.
This is where the world seems only to rise
behind leather gloves, as we clear trails,
rebuild the cairns above the treeline,
pack tins of food to the fire stations,
where we hear the voice that says
we have never gone far enough,
that we should never go back down,
that we should just vanish up here like fog
in the morning over the notches.
When it rains, we will sit in the tent
and try to remember our parents' faces,
the way as children we slept in back seats
on long drives from the sea.
We will not listen to that voice.
We will remind each other that people
once wore blindfolds against mountains
they believed would drive them mad.

THE RELOCATION
OF RATTLESNAKES

Once they lay everywhere.
You'd turn over a bucket and there'd be
that cool smile, a muscular rippling
through the coiled body.
Or beneath the porch, slats of light
over a flat head with its fangs
and fissures and sacs of poison.
We learned how to walk lightly
through that slow gathering of mottled skin
sliding soundlessly over dry leaves.

They were a spell over the landscape,
heat seeking, drawn to rock outcrops
that all night radiated sun.
They stretched across hot macadam roads.
Sometimes we'd find one dead on the berm
or draped over a wire fence.
Then one day they disappeared.
Someone had come in the night
with burlap bags and hooked sticks,
and plucked them one by one.
We searched the hedgerows,
pushed aside ferns, looked under the porch.

What did we have without
that slithering ease, those warnings?

We'd grow heavy, careless,
sink into ourselves. We'd no longer
gather each spring to watch them crawl
out of the cave above the river.
How will we sleep
now that the landscape is so safe?
They were a border of coil and strike
we might never again cross.

THE WEATHER STONE

For Steve and Donald

It hung in one corner of our dirt cellar,
surrounded by spider webs,
and looked a little like a spear point.

If you touched it, nothing happened,
but it was the weather stone,
and sometimes turned a darker gray,
and sometimes twisted, though no wind
blew in that place.

Sometimes it smelled of caves,
sometimes of rain on dusty flowers,
but never of the other weather
that drifted past sofa and piano,
and over knuckles and African violets.

What did it matter we lived in two,
maybe three different places,
us in our brogans with metal cleats,
and our mackinaws?
                    All that hissing
and shrieking, the sweet faces
that kissed us, the stone that warned us.

PORCH

This is the evening I have finished
the screened porch my father
always promised her.

He stole two-by-fours, nails,
a roll of screen from the colliery,
but never had the time,
always whistling off around Sammy's corner
and calling back to her,
Tomorrow you'll have the damned thing.

Out she comes,
dry dough under her fingernails,
slowing when she sees the porch,
her old round table, some books,
a view over the red barn
and up Kohler's Hill.

She lays her hand flat against the screen.
She smoothes her dress beneath her
and sits in the wicker chair.
She notices evening primrose
and the last celandine along the swale.
He would have done it, she says. *He would.*

LANDSCAPE WITH OLGA

Our town was pinched in the middle because the mountains
to the north and south bulged inward. You could tell the
time to the second just by standing there and listening to the
old women in babushkas whispering as they slouched by on
their way to mass at St. Vincent's. They all smelled of blood
sausage, blind pigeons, halupkies. They'd stare at us. We'd
stare back. We'd throw rocks at them as they climbed the
church steps. We could hear their knees scraping the cold
floor close to the altar. *In hoc signo vinces,* we would shout.
We'd read that on our fathers' cigarette packages. There was
a dead calm where the town narrowed that we could stand
for only so long. Who needed such a pinched sense of time?
It was summer. Down the alley in the wide part of town lived
Olga, the timeless beauty we could stare at and not feel like
throwing rocks. She'd stand on the porch as we walked back
and forth. Wind ruffled her long skirt. Her mother would
come out and curse us in Polish. Nights we'd hide in the
shadows below the railroad tracks. Dogs would growl. A light
would go on in Olga's kitchen, chickens clucked nervously.
Someone yelled, Go on, you boys, get away from here. Go
on home, your mother's calling. We snickered, we were in
love. We could hardly believe our luck when a crumpled note
fell from her bedroom window. We soon found out about
luck. We soon found out about love. Everywhere we walked
the ground seemed to open beneath our feet. Then we grew
up, stopped playing basketball, and stood around on street
corners until it was time to leave for the Army. One of us
wore a cross while the rockets roared over. One of us mar-
ried a girl named Olga, but from another town. One of us
kept the note and spent a lifetime hoping to understand.

Lee & Melissa, Always

It begins like this, names spray-painted
on a piling beneath an interstate bridge,
and the *always* they believe in
and count on so much, years of it,
after high school, hot nights of each other,
cold beers and rowboats at the lake,
sand shaken from towels long after midnight.
It's this *always* I keep coming back to.
Suppose they did find it.
Suppose they were out walking one day
past an empty ramshackle house,
and suddenly there was someone
hammering a sign into the brown grass
that even as they watched turned deep green,
and the porch banister nailed in place,
baskets of ferns, rocking chairs, a swing,
the whole house freshly painted.
The *always* would always be there,
the salesman said, putting his hammer down,
reaching into his pocket for the keys,
always children at the perfect age,
always May or mid-June, bags always packed
and in the hallway, ready for the drive
to the seashore. Lee, she would call out.
Melissa, he would answer from the garden
where he'd just looked up from the lettuce
at some purple clouds like names

he could not quite read in the light,
the light always just a little too sharp
for understanding any of it.
What really happened, for example,
that night he was out alone,
driving around dirt roads and blacktops,
taking turns too fast, and once
skidding into a cornfield, until at last
he stopped in the cool darkness
beneath the bridge, and with steady hands
made his faithful, his only mark.

THE VISIT

Isn't it beautiful, she'd say,
meaning the maples and the stream,
the breeze every once in a while,
and her with her bad eyes and dark glasses
seeing it clearly as ever,
reaching out to me, patting my arm.

Isn't it, she'd say again, the years
lightly on her as she started
across the board we used in the beginning
for a bridge, a teeter-totter
that made her laugh, saying no no
when we reached out to her,

and then safely down on the other side,
off to inspect hollyhocks and mock orange,
and us following along behind, quiet,
reverential, as if a spirit
had wandered into our garden
and was naming things for the first time.

EDWARD HOPPER'S WOMEN·

Looking away is what they do best.
They sit in full sunlight,
their knees pulled up to their breasts.

They seem to shiver
from sharp shadows on a granite wall
or that train entering a tunnel.

What's beyond them is hard to imagine.
Enough mystery for a lifetime.
You think they've missed out on everything.

Not one of them is about
to take a step away or scream for help.
What could you possibly say to them?

WOMAN WITH ALLIGATOR

What muddy writhing and roaring
there must have been when her bullet struck,
what biting on nothing at all.
Now it hangs from a tree,
tail almost touching the ground,
the tip of its jaws run through with wire.
Light strikes the Himalaya of its back.
The slitted eyes turn away
from the pond where nightly
it prowled shallows
or lay quietly among water lilies,
only those eyes and nostrils
showing above the surface.

So this is how it works now,
this stiffening, this obscene posture,
this photograph, the woman
dressed in tweeds the color
of the alligator's skin,
the skin soon to be peeled away,
the assembly of tissues
and pits and blood
thrown out to turtles and fish,
instinct no longer circling the dark,
skin softened and dyed, sewn up,
fit for a lilac-scented drawer.

NATURE

When our friend's wife forgot
and walked right through the screen door,
you remembered your father
breaking into your house with a gun,
the red lights and bull horns,
the three children huddled in a corner,
your mother whimpering.
You said, Let's drink to fathers.
It was honeysuckle time,
lilacs and wild roses.
Dusk drifted over the deck,
woods filled up with shadows.
I remembered a father
holding his daughter up to a black bear
so the bear could lick jam
from the little girl's face,
the mother taking movies.
You remembered a Russian movie
about an unmarried clerk
whose new overcoat was stolen,
an empty, snow-filled night
and the clerk's terrible screams.
It reminded you of a painting,
a quay, a violent sunset,
two ships, two walkers going away,

and a man with a head like a skull,
his hands drawn close along his face,
his eyes and mouth wide open,
who had seen something, or heard.
As later in the evening,
after the door was back on its track,
and our friend's wife had dried her eyes,
she said something quietly to her husband
who had already turned away.

ADULTERY

One day she comes home with no coat,
the next no shoes. Friday a week,
no purse, no gloves. I blame her father,
her minister, her teachers.
I wonder did she leave pom poms
in the library, cheers and saddle shoes
near the school bus stop?
Years of her years forgotten in shops,
backs seats of cars, in gaps
left by marriages of friends,
the deaths of aunts, uncles,
the crazy grandfather.

Even now I imagine her
coming down the street, fingers and elbows
left behind on windowsill or table,
arch and instep and ankle
still poised above a curb.
Her mouth misplaces its sounds
in public restrooms,
forming the zeros of loss exactly,
blouse, brassiere, the brown skirt falling away.

I imagine her opening buttons,
zippers, clasps, clips,
stepping out of the circle
of slip and panties,
moving like a drift of absence
through the half-light of attic and basement.

I blame her doctor, her sisters,
her love of bones, things Jurassic,
names of reptiles, her dreams
of seeing them all alive again
by swamp or tar pit.
I blame laughter,
the invisible hands on ass and belly,
hands removing hair ribbon and suede vest.

I imagine this:
          that she has forgotten
her eyes, her skin and ovaries, her vagina,
that she rattles some,
attracts a final stare or two,
that if I could see her asleep
there would be no rise and fall
of breast, no line of spittle
on her chin, that behind her
are men with brooms and bags,
that not even a small moan escapes her
as she turns a corner at dusk
and perfectly, perfectly,
becomes the final thing left behind.

Throwing Away
the Compass

the streets led the usual way back
there was no reason to suspect
a god was angry and on the prowl
until the sky tilted and buildings folded
suddenly I was up to my blood
in all of it and going down
for maybe the last time
sinking in the most familiar straits of all
everywhere the world led was flat
and full of distance only nearby
first a hand then an arm shyly a face
the body soft in almost imagined beauty
came toward me bearing in delicate
swirls a shawl of sorts and left
I floated for days her eyes everywhere
her love still wrapped around my waist
when I reached at last a place
near home and came ashore dripping
with relief I should have remembered
to thank her at least for my life
though for her love there could be
no turning not a single look back.

Fishing at Dusk

Comes my tipsy father,
hurrying me past the cemetery
to the stream rippling through pools
in the last hour or so of light.

We head for his favorite place below the bridge
where honeysuckle hangs low,
where we cast into the shadows over stones
that seem to have names and dates.

It is early October.
My father drifts in and out of view,
taking his time putting a worm on the hook
and some weight on the leader.

He has brought a lantern and beer.
Never you mind, he says,
and then he says something else,
a little cooler, farther away.

Giacometti's Trout

Maybe in Paris I watched it
lying under a rock shelf.

Sometimes it had thin legs
and heavy feet, sometimes wheels.

November's ashen light
streamed over gill slits

and where the eyes used to be.
It could have been

a drawing on a cave wall
a gallery of skin and bones,

a thin braid of either hunger or rage,
of gasps and splotches,

a few short seasons
flowing past sycamores

and stone walls.
Small boys chased it.

They wanted to hang it
on a chain.

A woman put on lipstick
and rouge

and picked up a frying pan.
Each morning

it floated past open windows
and left no trail.

My Daughter Snorkeling

One more world
you entered on your own,
adjusting the mask, slipping off
face down through the water,
circling the dock,
breath tube sticking straight up,
a slow progression
over the sunken slime-coated tree,
a bottle, a fishing weight,
shimmer and play of light.
Waves broke softly over you.
A damselfly landed on your hair.
If you went out too far,
this was to be the signal:
two stones clicked together underwater
and you would turn back to us,
still easy enough, still dependable.

WHY NOT SWIM OUT

to the boat we've been looking at
for two days through fog and rain,
and climb aboard, the two of us
putting our heads together at the controls,
the starter button, gauges, the wheel.
Somewhere on the water
it's bound to clear, out past Gull Island,
say, with its spindly trees and absence of gulls,
far beyond the weathers of this house.
Let's cruise in and out of every inlet,
naming them after cats and dogs we've buried.
Let's stop for a drink on the porch
of the ramshackle house
with its five chimneys and its line-up
of vultures each morning, their wings spread,
waiting for wind to lift them off.
Let's roar in and out of fog banks,
hanging on joyously and for dear life,
returning with news of what we've found.

GUESTS

My mother raises her eyes to heaven,
and whispers, *Love of Jesus,*

here they come again,
my two sweet uncles, drunk

and stomping up our back steps,
laughing, tilting their heads back.

And always the two of them the same way
whether at a funeral or a picnic,

saying to my mother, *God love you, Dorse,*
there's nothing like what comes off

that black Maria of a stove of yours.
And her giving it right back,

saying they weren't fit to walk
the length of a spoon, a disgrace.

The two of them sitting there,
heads down, hands in their laps,

as if she were saying grace
instead of stirring things up.

RAVEN RUN COAL BREAKER

Soot-stained, every glass pane smashed,
a cenotaph filled with pigeons
cooing from high catwalks,
corrugated iron walls rusted through.

Over there a railroad bed,
truck tires, cables, the dirt road
winding past orange water, spill banks,
pink laurel blossoms.

Once you could see blurred faces
behind begrimed windows,
and feel the pound and thump
of big spiked rollers shattering lumps of coal.

Voices and faces have been lost in dust,
dust sifting into row homes
and over cups and saucers,
the whole place a gigantic raving chimney

until there was nothing left
to be sucked into its blackened guts
except a dry hacking cough,
breath taken away.

CARRYING WATER
TO THE MINER

He'd be sitting at the top
of the bootleg hole, beneath the tipple
with its iron chute,

the big REO backed up beneath it.
I was just old enough to know
about falling, and not to be afraid

of his coal-darkened face. Every time
he'd have a little something for me,
a fern fossil or fossilized piece

of wood, a sulfur diamond,
that after he'd had his drink
he place in my hand, his gritty

bruised hand against mine,
and the smell of that deep place on him
that I'd carry all the way home.

DROUGHT CHRONICLE

Below the almost empty reservoir,
on a stone rip-rap, dozens of watersnakes,
copperheads and rattlesnakes
lay in the August sun, the cicada's cry
rising over their chilly smiles.

If I believed strongly enough
I could walk among them.
I could reach down and touch
the most venomous, handle them,
kiss their eyes and pits, drape them over my arm,

remembering one that crushed
and swallowed my father's prize pigeon,
that he shot where it slept coiled
in a corner of the coop,
then hacked it open and took out the bird,

cursing, hurling the snake high
into a mulberry where it hung for months,
bits of it falling with faint hisses.
Think of a sinewy fellowship
that grows more alert the hotter it becomes,

a ripening of beauty and grace,
while everything else sags and shrivels,
even the sky. I tap my stick against rock,
hoping for one head to turn my way,
to have its flicking tongue find me out.

The Reply to Oregon

When the letter arrived from Oregon, our father would come out of his February gloom and silence. The envelope was covered with cartoon figures, Cupids, red lips. He'd slip it into his pocket and walk upstairs where we'd hear him laughing, stamping his foot, and playing a tin whistle. We looked at our mother. Where's Oregon? we asked. She hitched her thumb over her shoulder toward the end of Ash Alley where the slush flats began. Our mother had been a teacher. Our father dug for coal in a hole and had blue scars on his face and right hand. His February love letter, our mother said, as she rolled out a perfect circle of dough. A red-flecked pigeon sat outside the window. There were yellow lights in all the row homes on our block. If we put our ears to the wall by the steps, we could hear our father quietly weeping, trying to find the words for his reply.

GAME

Two of us would be given a head start,
the others counting to a hundred.
This was up on the slag banks
overgrown with sumac and white birch.
Big slabs of slate stood on end,
some tipped over, making little caves.
We had to watch out for places
where a mine tunnel had caved-in
and left a jagged hole straight down.
We took our time at first, picking our way,
careful not to overturn piles of leaves
or leave behind muddied puddles.

Then something else took over
that sent us racing flat out,
stumbling, branches lashing our faces,
both of us listening for shouts,
clatter of rock slides set off to flush us out,
lungs burning, mouths dry,
not even looking for places to hide,
not even splitting up as we crashed
toward the old mine road that curved
down the mountain, past water-filled pits,
dumps of rusted cables, tires, tin cans, bottles,
and all the time the others gaining,
spreading out, sticks up to their shoulders,
taking careful aim.

LOCUSTS

One morning they were all over town,
a whine, a shrillness rising
from branches and porch rails.
We went after them with broomsticks
and rolled-up newspapers, the ground
and sidewalks littered with crushed bodies,
some crawling crookedly off.
Rats came up from sewers in broad daylight,
feasting, that we also attacked.

Good boys, our fathers said.
Our mothers swept dry husks into gutters.

It lasted for weeks, then they were gone,
but in seventeen years
they'd come back from down there,
a man told us, pointing at the ground.

And were they in the mine tunnels
where our fathers worked?
And was it vengeance
caused rock slip or pillar to collapse,
that brought some neighboring house to grief?

The Double

He would have loved it here
on the screened porch, the mimosa
with its catbird a few feet away,

and maybe he'd walk down to the dock,
letting his bare feet dangle
in the out-going tide,

and the sky the way it gets
this far south, just the color
of the blue coal scars on his face.

So he gives the old thumbs up,
as if to say you've done all right for yourself
since the days on Ash Alley,

and then lifts an imaginary shotgun
at five geese honking by.
I can almost see the recoil

against his shoulder, then again,
a double, his eye as good as ever.

NEW DARK

I walk into the ocean,
trying not to think
of the drive back in two days
to the house we are leaving,
and the new one we'll move into,
the house on top of the hill
with its absence of trees,
the house like a pueblo
that faces south,
that I will be lonely in,
my balance lost,
no longer recognizing
the constellations,
nor ways into blackberry bushes
or into deer feeding
in the L-shaped evening field,
the ocean cold
against my legs,
the bottom shifting,
and me thinking ahead
to winter nights,
snow over Thistle Hill,
learning the new dark.

SMALL HISTORY
OF A HOUSE

One late May afternoon
two black snakes
still wrapped around each other,
pushed in their mating frenzy
through a heating vent
in the ceiling and fell at my feet,
landing unhurt with a soft thud
and lay still, still twined together.
I closed the door on them
and went for a burlap bag and leather gloves.
Imagine, ten feet of black snakes
coiled around your arms.
I put them into the bag
and carried it to the sunny side of the barn.

When I went back in the morning
they were gone. I like to think
of them as fog, drifting into our house
through foundation or some opening
I do not know about into the attic,
and slipping over our heads,
small rustlings that make us look up,
that sound like bits of plaster
falling from laths, or something else
we almost recognize, a way
of moving toward love
or that place where we simply fall.

HER MORNING

Once each year she comes back,
softly across our back porch,
bare arms lifted
toward maple and oak
with their first green hue,
clouds of pollen drifting
over blackbirds and finch,
slowly turning the way she did
so many years ago,
whispering my name, my father's,
her lips thin and steady as the horizon,
but oh how startling
to see again the way she leaves,
blue eyes catching
the sun risen above the ridge,
her red hair tangled
in the hawthorn's red blossoms.

DANCE HALL

This is my sister walking down the wooden steps
to the wet sand and the greenheads,
her handkerchief balled in her hand.
She might be gone all morning,
walking as far as the abandoned fish factory,
maybe sitting among the bricks
and rusty nails, maybe talking
to the oystercrackers and terns
or wading the shallows with the rays
and the horseshoe crabs,
wiping her good eye
and forgetting the missing one,
finding the plover's nest on the gravel
with its small eggs the color
of weathered wood, my sister
having a good time, clapping her hands
also the color of plover eggs,
remembering jitterbug and Johnny Ray,
and her two young daughters,
the silence, her broken fingernails,
cursing the empty dance hall.

Leah in the Outfield

What is she thinking in right field,
doing her little two step,
the glove like some shy part of herself
at the ready with each pitch?

All that space, the loneliness
that she hustles out to each inning,
thirteen, her team losing,
not even sure she likes the game,
how nothing happens, its lasting hurts.

There will come years, fly balls
of long afternoons and evenings
with red and purple clouds, leaves turning up
in a breeze, a shadow slanted over bleachers.

Think of it. Buckner at Shea,
Emily Dickinson in her room,
Ishmael drifting back to tell us what went wrong.

HAND-ME-DOWNS

Someone has piled hundreds of dead bees on the kitchen table that the breeze pushes one way, then another. We watched them all afternoon while a woman lengthened or shortened corduroy pants. It was homecoming for the boys of the town who'd gone away to grow up and who had not been back in twenty years. Honeysuckle filled the air. A musty secret hung over the bees. What could we possibly say to the boys who had grown moustaches and leaned on laurel sticks? One was missing an arm. Another remembered the exact place he'd buried a dog. They recognized the bees as something exhumed from their childhood, and turned away, their faces hidden in blue-scarred hands. They spoke either Latin or a rough English. What? What? we kept asking. We followed them all around town. They'd look back and make jokes about our clothes. Flood pants, they yelled. Shitkickers, they snorted. We turned away. Who were they anyway to be talking? Look at their mismatched lives and turned-out pockets after all those years at Tastykake and Ford. Who did they think they were kidding? A bunch of bozos with neither chick nor child, back for some fried chicken and red potato salad. Home to say hello to mothers they no longer recognized. Then without warning the bees were all gone. Not on the ground where the wind might have blown them, not mixed in with pebbles the same faded color and shape, even down to the dried-out stinger. An infestation of mites in the hives, someone said. A shabby catechism of bees, a vanishing of bees, a tragedy of bees. For days we yelled out at the growling dogs to be quiet. Maybe it was winter by then, maybe the night before Christmas. The boys had gone back across the river. Coal popped in the stove. All of us stood by the side window.

TROUT ARE MOVING

Past midnight they slip free
of pools and deep runs, they rise

above thistle down and meadow dew,
hover in eddies of slate roof and chimney,

drifting through window and hallway,
gill flare and eye sweep

above pillow and comforter
and over the gravelly dark,

here and there a run of moonlight,
a swirl of pale mayflies

as if risen from a sleeper's easy breath,
and all that time holding steady,

crimson side spots, once in a while
a slow shiver of backbone,

a shimmering, until in the first
up-welling of light through maple and ash,

suddenly a trail of bubbles
along a fin edge, not even

an easy turning around
nor that quick back and forth panic

when a trout is startled,
just a sinking away

through the ordinary stillness
of the house.

The Stream

For Rachel

We were always listening to it,
wondering what it was saying to the rocks.

Smoke drifted from our fire
over swirls and gravel.

It was shadow and gurgle,
a dazzle of light that shocked us

when we dipped our hands.
Even when we hiked miles away,

it seemed all around us.
We were there and not there,

the two of us, in that singing place,
sitting up late, crayons and tablets,

white moths fluttering at the lantern,
and just beyond us, out there

in the dark flowing past . . .
Listen, can you still hear it?

CRAB LINES

Four of them in a box I'd forgotten,
wrapped around pieces of driftwood,
frayed, knotted here and there,
and at the end of each that big safety pin
to hang a chicken neck on,
then giving it a swing out over the water
the way he showed us,
as I do again this morning,
the line sailing over the field,
remembering slack tides, and him
telling us they were like pieces
of the bottom broken free
and swimming sideways,
always hungry, big blue claws
ready to latch on to anything.
You'd feel their little tugs through the line,
and slowly pull them in,
hand over hand, and them refusing
to let go, hanging on all the way
to the long-handled net,
sometimes two or three at a time.
So this morning from goldenrod and thistle
the tug of his *Easy does it, easy now.*

CLAM GATHERER

He moves across the mud flats,
a red handkerchief around his head,

a tin water bottle tied to his belt,
towing a bushel basket on an inner tube.

He is on vacation from his tunnels,
his body pale and bruised.

We are too far away to hear him whistling
or smell gas bubbles rising

around him when he rakes bottom muck.
He rinses the clams, juggles

a few, dances his small dance,
spins and splashes, goes under,

his hands flashing above the surface.
He could be a loggerhead turtle

taking forever to come ashore,
his mouth clear of dust, cough gone,

waving to cormorants sitting on stumps
drying their outstretched wings,

waving to plovers on their gravel nests.
Afternoon filters through him,

and dazzles and gleams
over his wake and the basket's wake,

over the clatter of clams in a pot,
the tide of us around the big table.

EVOLUTION

For weeks, half a dozen mockingbirds,
squawked and dove at the cats,
tangled with each other in midair.
Sitting, they resemble dinosaurs.
It's their eyes, I think,
that sleek shape from beak to tail.
They attack cardinals and goldfinch.
They mimic the cry of red-tailed hawks.
I go to a closet and take out
my old .22, and go back to the porch,
remembering years before,
cocky, too sure of myself,
the same rifle in hand, walking
to the town dump to wait for rats
to come out of their holes
after putrid meat and cheese
thrown out by the A&P,
their gray humpbacked shapes moving
along trails through piles of coal ash,
boxes, tires, and bottles.
Just one of the birds, I think,
then hang it from the porch,
a reminder to the others
that who lives in this house,
still has a steady eye
and trigger finger, and still loves
the cool feel of a cartridge,

the slight click when one slides
into the chamber, the jerk
against a shoulder, and then the curl
of smoke from the barrel,
smoke almost the color
of the bird's white wing bars,
the bird in the crosshairs,
the one with a red chokecherry
in its beak, the one who coolly stares
back from millions of years away,
the one who flies over my head and away.

A THEORY

They have gathered this late afternoon
at the end of October,
the swallows Linnaeus thought slept
all winter beneath ice,
legs tucked up,
their glistening purple
and white covered with gravel.
They circle the lake after bugs,
then dive to sip the water,
leaving circles that break
softly against the shore.
Why not at such a time
believe in them folding their wings
and slipping beneath the surface?
Why not let a season and its sadness
be dealt with simply as that,
with hardly a splash at all?

THE RIVER IS
QUIET TONIGHT

An easy weave of light and shadow
over bottom rock, green fading
to gray, riffle whisper and trout flash,
easy to wade with the mink
and small green heron, the water snake,
away from things, not even fishing,
picking up a red leaf, a white feather,
trailing a hand in the water
like all the other hands, a father's
with blue coal scars, a grandfather's hook
that he'd run through my hair,
a mother's dough-clotted fingernails,

remembering shyness and sorrow,
the row house that leaned
to one side because of mine subsidence,
smells of bread and potatoes,
wet feathers and oil cloth,
pigeons circling slush banks,
the black DeSoto by the curb,

more than can be remembered near water,
though that is always a good place to begin,

with the geese coming in,
their black feet stretched out,
and tilted up just before they hit,
then settling wings into place,
if anything a kind of music,
a kind of prayer at evening.

The Stillness

And after the slap of water
against a passing canoe and those five geese,
their wings whistling past pine and mimosa,
it was as if a door had opened
and it was Sunday and you were saying
how nice it was and wouldn't the Mister
have enjoyed himself here,
this big porch near the water.
Can't you just see him?
Both arms crossed on the rail,
chin propped on them, and him quiet as always,
maybe humming, ready to go whenever we were.

ANTLER TREE

One night I will sneak across the alfalfa
and along the stream to my neighbor's house,
to the antlers, their whiteness
catching moonlight,
and run my fingers along skull plates and tines,
loosen the nails,
and take them to the overgrown orchard,
leaving them beneath apple trees
for the mice, the brown thrasher
to rest on, for whatever else
might come along and softly cover.

Carved Animals
in My Room

Their eyes never burn yellow or red.
They lay no eggs in sand nor spill air
from beneath wings.
They leave no spoor or splash.
No twig snaps beneath a paw.
The bear that strides
across the salmon's back
will never tear its flesh.
The wren's tail is always still,
the fox's jaw never opens,
and the crows never attack.
They frighten no one,
disturb nothing.
They remain in their bloodless instant.
They will never wake
into moonlight streaming
over woods and tall grass.

August Evening
with Trumpet

Up in the woods a neighbor or stranger
who has had enough of August,
its spider webs and first yellow

near the roots of things,
has out of the blue found his old voice,
wailing away everything

he can remember.
Perhaps he will play
right through fall and winter,

not stopping until bloodroot
and anemone blossom.
But now it is almost dark.

Mist veils the fields,
and last sounds play out
as simply as longing or breath.

In Different Form

Morning light glitters along spider webs
and the chokecherry branches we cut last night,
and over the Adirondack chair.
                                        The foggy hills
seem farther off and the cicada's cry shorter.

Now a swallowtail, a sulfur,
a hummingbird, a turtle lumbering
toward the swamp.
                                Everything sharply edged,
more precisely there, though smaller and cooler.

Beneath our feet, a catechism plain and simple
as the snap of a dry stick.

Gravel Song

You were born in a suitcase, our mother would tell us. She'd
be standing at the stove, stirring a pot of stew or frying fish on
Meatless Friday. A suitcase, she'd say, and go on stirring and
smiling. Our mother loved trains and Tycho Brahe. She'd tell
us he had no nose and had made one out of silver. She guessed
that nose was as cold as the heavens Tycho Brahe was always
prowling around in. We'd prowl around in the attic cubby hole
and take out the brown suitcase. It was tied with a belt that
had no buckle. Inside was a safety pin and a postcard from
Atlantic City of a horse jumping off a tower. We asked her if
it was the one we were born in? She smiled again, picked some
dried flour dough off her fingernails. That very one, she said.

At the town dump we'd smash bottle after bottle with a
broomstick. Rats looked out of their holes, whiskers twitching,
their eyes like nail heads. We'd walk with our father as far as
the railroad trestle, but he would never let us cross it with
him, never let us walk up the dirt path. He'd grow smaller
and smaller and then vanish into the opening in the side of
the mountain where he dug for coal. One day he came home
groaning and coughing up black-streaked phlegm, his hands
and face covered with dirt. He limped and held one twisted
arm ahead of him. His hair was singed. Our mother wept
into the handkerchief she pulled from her left sleeve. We'll
pack the suitcase and leave, she said, her words sounding like
my tin shovel when I scraped it across gravel. But we never
went anywhere.

BASHO

So here it is again, same as last time,
water under the bridge, a day straight
as the crow flies, and light
smoky through the woods.

There is no other color except brown and gray,
and a rattling from the tree
whose leaves do not fall.
                              Oh,
so this is what you meant
when you mentioned
a weather into which we'd drift
one afternoon late in November.

WALKING BY THE OCEAN

When he felt the sand tremble
and give way beneath him, he stepped back,
thinking here it was at last,
the stuff of his childhood nightmares,
the ooze into which Frankenstein's monster sank,
and from which the Mummy rose
with hands trailing wet wrappings.
He circled it, that place
with different tensions and tricks of gravity.
If he had two boards, he could strap
them to his feet and walk out over it.
He could fish around
and put an ear close in case it spoke
as earth used to.
He put a warning at the edge,
but did not kid himself,
knowing it would not stop the damage,
the steady sinking into the world.

LATE NOVEMBER

Its front leg caught in a steel trap,
the raccoon had torn the ground with its struggle,
and growled and rattled its teeth
when I lowered my coat over its head,
one hand pushing down on the coat,
the other forcing a stick between the trap's jaws.
They opened just enough for the leg to pull loose,
the leg almost chewed through,
the leg from which hung shreds of skin and fur.
I pulled away the coat and the raccoon stumbled off,
stopping once to lick the wound,
then splashed across the stream.
Blood swirled downstream.
Water dripped from belly fur.
What was it found me after the raccoon vanished
into thick multiflora rose? A hand
or words pushing against my eyes,
out of myself for a few minutes,
my mind like a failed theory.
Next to me, the white peels and splotches
of the sycamore rose into the sky.
Lower down, nothing had changed.

AN IRRUPTION
OF BIRDS

All of us sick of winter,
of darkness, the sun stalled
along Grim's Ridge, days
of ice and wind,
                    and then
one morning dropped from some
frozen place worse than ours
came Pine Siskins
with yellow tail feathers,

Grosbeaks with white wing bars,
Crossbills, Redpolls, and Nuthatch,
dark eyes, feather blur,
bobbing on dry yarrow stalks,

some at feeders, a smokeless
burning, a frenzy of air,
though none of it stirring
over us light or warmth,

nor in all the spherical order
was there sign of anything else.

PLOWED FIELDS
IN JANUARY

Last night's rain froze over them
and now they are ocean
waves seen a long way off, glittering
and clicking, the wind carrying
scent of flotsam and jetsam,
then spindrift and coils of fog,
that all morning move on their own melting,
teasing the eye, the blood,
until as if a great wave has poured through
comes a spilling of ice from crest
to furrow, and suddenly
the fields lie becalmed, bare,
though still tidal and cold,
still deep.

THE MOVEMENT
OF ICE

What comes, comes from the south
as if a gate had been left unlatched,
and an eye blinked open,
                              something
that gathered itself, that all night
made no noise slipping and curling

over gully and hedgerow, hissing past
a kitchen window.
                              Finch and bluejay
do not flutter when it brushes
over their feathers.
                              It is in no hurry.
It cannot be stopped.
                              If you lose your way,
it will leave you lying huddled and stung.

It does not dazzle nor inspire,
nor bludgeon nor badger, has no claw.

It leaves a trail a child can follow.

It softens all edges,
                              its entrails gray-blue
outlines of what was once familiar,

the back of your hand, a path behind the shed,
a ridge of pines.

                It moves in all directions.

It moves the way you remember a girl
in a shimmery dress moving

as she walked toward you through music,
laughing.

              It was summer 1968,
and she was holding out her arms.